TIM A. MARS

Overcoming Relationship Anxiety and Overthinking Book

Navigating the Maze of Emotions

Contents

Introduction

Welcome to "Overcoming Relationship Anxiety and Overthinking," a book that aims to inspire you to forge better bonds with the people you care about while assisting you in negotiating the tricky waters of relationships.

Whether you are in a romantic partnership, a friendship, or any other form of interpersonal connection, this book is meant to offer insights, practical strategies, and support to help you break free from the grip of anxiety and overthinking that may be holding you back.

Relationships are an important aspect of the human experience, bringing joy, fulfillment, and a feeling of belonging. However, they can also be a source of discomfort, causing feelings of insecurity, doubt, and fear. You are not alone if you frequently overthink situations, question your partner's goals, or worry about the future of your relationship. Many individuals struggle with relationship anxiety and overthinking, and it can be a formidable job to overcome without proper guidance.

This book tries to shed light on the causes of relationship anxiety and overthinking in order to help you understand the elements that contribute to these patterns. By going back in time and thinking about how the things that happened in the past affect our actions today, you can discover a lot about the reasons behind your anxiety. You can start your journey toward healing and change now that you are armed with this information.

You will learn useful techniques and tools for managing and decreasing relationship anxiety on these pages. You will learn to control your emotions more carefully by building mindfulness and self-awareness as well as rewiring unhelpful thought patterns. Additionally, you will find help on stress management and how to deal with anxiety episodes, empowering you to regain control over your emotional responses.

Moreover, this book emphasizes the significance of building healthy and nurturing relationships. We explore the important elements of trust, communication, and emotional intimacy, providing you with the tools to improve your connections with others. Whether you are trying to rebuild trust after a betrayal or improve emotional closeness with your partner, you will find valuable strategies to create a solid basis for your relationships.

Recognizing that long-distance relationships come with their own unique set of challenges, this book also dedicates a section to address the special concerns faced by people in such situations. From keeping trust and connection across distances to making long-distance relationships work, we provide insights to help you handle the complexities with confidence.

While this book tries to provide guidance and practical tips, it also acknowledges the value of getting professional help when needed. We discuss the benefits of couples therapy and offer tips on how to find the right therapist to support your journey toward healthier relationships.

As you begin on this journey of self-discovery and growth, remember that overcoming relationship anxiety and overthinking is a process. Be patient and compassionate with yourself as you handle the challenges and enjoy the wins, no matter how small they may seem. You are not defined by your anxiety; instead, you hold the power to create the satisfying and happy relationships you desire.

So, let's begin on this ever-changing journey together. Turn the page, open your mind, and prepare to welcome a life free from the shackles of relationship worry and overthinking. Your way to healthier, happier relationships starts now.

Chapter One: Understanding Relationship Anxiety and Overthinking

The core concepts of relationship anxiety and overthinking are examined in this chapter, and we learn more about how they impact our relationships and daily lives. By comprehending the intricacies of these emotions, we start the process of releasing their hold on us and open the way for enlightened self-reflection.

What is Relationship anxiety?

Relationship anxiety is a complicated emotional response that manifests in the area of interpersonal relationships and has a big impact on how we view and manage our interactions with others. It encapsulates a variety of feelings, such as anxiety, doubt, and unease, and frequently results from an underlying worry about the sustainability and future of a romantic relationship or any other type of personal connection. Each manifestation of this complex emotional state provides insight into the nuances of psychological processes and human emotions.

The constant worry that a person has about the stability of their relationship is a significant example of relationship anxiety. This anxiety could manifest as unceasing worries about possible issues, disagreements, or even the probability that the relationship would fail. People who struggle with this type of anxiety may get fixated on "what if" situations and continually over-analyze their partner's words and actions for any indication of problems. This constant state of uncertainty can increase one's sense of vulnerability and unease, making it challenging to completely engage in the relationship without the nagging shadow of uncertainty looming in the distance.

Furthermore, severe rejection anxiety, which can be crippling in both new and established relationships, is another manifestation of relationship anxiety. The dread of being abandoned or rejected by a relationship can cause anything from mild insecurity to severe anxiety. People with this kind of anxiety may find it difficult to be candid with their relationships because they have a deep-seated worry of not being accepted for who they really are. This can make it difficult for people to effectively communicate and can create an environment where people are emotionally distant because they are unable to articulate their wants and desires.

Another aspect of relationship anxiety is the overpowering need for unceasing reassurance. People who struggle with this component of anxiety frequently go to great lengths to feel validated and affirmed by their partners, which may be extremely taxing for both parties. This constant need for affirmation may be a result of low self-esteem or a fear of inadequacy, which leads the person to place an excessive amount of weight on their partner's ideas and emotions.

Together, these relationship anxiety symptoms make it difficult to develop and maintain positive relationships with others. They frequently have roots in previous experiences, such as traumatic incidents or failed relationships, which might have an impact on current connections. Furthermore, underlying fears and a fear of vulnerability can amplify these anxieties, making it difficult for people to invest fully emotionally and forge long-lasting relationships.

Understanding the symptoms of relationship anxiety in ourselves and others is essential for promoting emotional health and personal development. People can start a journey of reflection and self-discovery by noticing and dealing with these uncomfortable feelings.

This procedure includes exploring the underlying roots of their concerns, facing earlier traumas, and developing self-compassion and self-assurance. Getting expert assistance, such as through therapy, can also give you vital direction and techniques to deal with these emotional difficulties.

Relationship anxiety is a complex emotional reaction that can manifest in many different ways, each of which affects our capacity to establish and keep deep relationships with others. We may foster personal development, healthier relationships, and more emotional resiliency by knowing the various ways that relationship anxiety presents itself and acknowledging its impact on our emotional health.

Identifying Overthinking Patterns

The cognitive activity of overthinking entails persistently analyzing and reflecting on numerous situations, events, or future outcomes. Overthinking may invade our minds like an unending flood. This complex mental activity frequently seems to be an infinite cycle of ideas that draws us farther into a maze of reflection. Overanalyzing can be a formidable foe in the world of relationships, throwing doubt on even the most promising ties. Thoughts can cause worry, insecurity, and a skewed perspective of reality as they swirl in an endless whirlwind.

Overthinking can be compared to a mental storm that forms in the setting of relationships. The emotions already present become more intense as the storm intensifies, frequently amplifying them to overwhelming levels.

This procedure may trigger a string of unfavorable ideas about various facets of the partnership. Overanalyzing people may agonize over perceived slights or mistakenly read benign statements as warning indications of disaster. Simply not receiving a text message right away can set off a series of speculative thoughts, each one more frightening than the previous.

Overthinking has the sneaky tendency to conjure up scenarios in the mind that are utterly unrepresentative of reality. Overthinkers are skilled at creating complex narratives based on scant information, frequently exaggerating small problems into large disasters. Because they contribute to a mistaken perception of one's partner and the relationship as a whole, these fictitious tales can be very harmful to relationships.

Overthinking is characterized by the cycle of rumination, which develops into a complex web that is challenging to break free of. An idea becomes more fixed and ingrained in someone's mind the more they ponder about it. As a result, their uneasiness and feelings of insecurity grow stronger. As the same thoughts keep coming back, breaking free of the cycle becomes increasingly difficult because each repetition puts more emotional strain on the person.

Gaining control of our thoughts and emotions requires that we become aware of the typical overthinking tendencies that occur in romantic relationships.

Catastrophizing, in which minor problems are exaggerated into catastrophic events, mind-reading, in which we assume that we know what our partner is thinking or feeling without concrete evidence, and all-or-nothing thinking, in which complex situations are reduced to absolutes—everything is either perfect or completely doomed—are examples of common overthinking patterns.

People might begin to recover control over their mental landscape by realizing how damaging overthinking is. To do this, one must develop self-awareness and learn to distinguish between useful and useless ruminating. Journaling, mindfulness, and cognitive-behavioral therapy are some useful strategies for escaping the cycle of overthinking and acquiring a more impartial view of relationships.

Relationship-related overthinking can exacerbate anxiety, warp perceptions, and impede emotional well-being. People can take the first important steps towards regaining control over their thoughts and emotions by becoming aware of the typical overthinking habits and their negative effects. This journey entails embracing self-awareness, acquiring healthier thought patterns, and cultivating a more forgiving and reasonable viewpoint on interpersonal relationships.

Overthinking and Relationship Anxiety's Effects on Your Life

It is essential to comprehend the extensive repercussions of relationship anxiousness and overthinking in order to spark transformational change. Despite appearing to be internal, these emotional states have a significant impact on many aspects of our lives, including our relationships, relationships with others, and our general quality of life. We can find the drive required to begin personal development and constructive change by exploring the negative effects of these emotions.

Mental and Emotional Health: It is impossible to overstate the toll that relationship worry and overthinking have on our mental and emotional health. These feelings can produce ongoing stress that raises our cortisol levels and sets off the body's fight-or-flight response. Rumination and concern are a vicious loop that can cause melancholy, anxiety disorders, and chronic stress. As our minds fill with unfavorable thoughts and images, our general emotional equilibrium becomes fragile, which limits our ability to experience joy and appreciate life.

Relationships: Overthinking and relationship anxiety can be damaging to the very relationships we value most. Trust and mutual understanding can be damaged by a propensity to constantly doubt the stability of a relationship or to read small-scale behaviors as warning indications of disaster. Additionally, the cycle of overthinking frequently results in irrational behavior, such as the need for ongoing confirmation or an exorbitant amount of justification from our relationships. Both parties may feel suffocated as a result of this behavior, which could drive lovers apart and lead to unneeded conflict.

Trust and intimacy: Overthinking and relationship anxiety can both seriously impair our capacity to have confidence in both ourselves and others. A foundation of trust cannot be built when we persistently mistrust the good intentions of our partners or question our own value. When we lack confidence in our own judgment and decision-making, it is difficult to manage relationships with assurance. As a result, we continue to be guarded and unable to really offer ourselves to vulnerability, which compromises our ability to have authentic connections.

Life Quality: Unchecked relationship anxiety and overthinking can have a negative impact on our general life quality. Our ability to be present in the moment and our ability to enjoy routine tasks can both be negatively impacted by the emotional weight of these states. As the mental load gets overwhelming, we could find it challenging to follow our interests, set personal objectives, or interact with others. Our entire sense of fulfillment and life happiness could decrease as a result.

The effects of relationship anxiety and overthinking in the real world can be clarified by using concrete examples and realistic circumstances. Imagine someone who is constantly afraid of being rejected and is unable to take chances or pursue meaningful relationships. Consider a scenario in which misinterpretations brought on by overanalyzing result in unnecessary conflict and animosity. a connection that could have otherwise thrived.

People gain the ability to make informed decisions by facing the effects of relationship anxiety and overthinking head-on. This self-awareness acts as a catalyst for transformation, encouraging people to get support, change their thought patterns, and practice self-compassion and mindfulness. In the end, overcoming these emotions' hold on us demands a dedication to personal development and a desire to build stronger, more rewarding relationships with both ourselves and others.

The first step in bringing about positive change is realizing the extensive impacts that relationship anxiety and overthinking have on our mental health, relationships, and quality of life. People can begin a journey of transformation and empowerment by recognizing how these emotions can cause self-sabotage, obstruct trust and intimacy, and negatively affect their general well-being. People who are self-aware and dedicated to improvement can progressively free themselves from the control of these emotions, resulting in healthier relationships and a more rewarding life path.

Chapter Two: Past Experiences and Their Influence on Present Relationships

Our past experiences play a significant role in shaping who we are and how we perceive and approach relationships. In this chapter, we explore how our past attachments and experiences affect the relationships we have today. We can learn a lot about the causes of relationship anxiety and overthink by investigating the emotional patterns that underlie them. With this knowledge in hand, we can begin to mend and transform our existing connections.

Exploring Childhood Attachments

Certainly, childhood lays the fundamental groundwork for our emotional development and the formation of our attachment styles, which in turn significantly influence our adult relationships. The early interactions and experiences we have with our caregivers play a pivotal role in shaping our perceptions of love, trust, and security. These perceptions are not confined to our childhood but tend to persist throughout our lives, impacting the way we connect with others in our intimate relationships.

Psychologists' attachment theory offers a framework for comprehending how these early experiences mold our attachment styles.

There are four main attachment styles: secure, anxious-preoccupied, dismissive-avoidant, and fearful-avoidant (also known as disorganized). Each of these styles arises from different combinations of our caregivers' responsiveness, consistency, and availability during our formative years.

Secure attachment is characterized by a healthy balance between independence and intimacy. Individuals with a secure attachment style tend to feel comfortable both being close to others and having their own space. They generally have positive beliefs about themselves and their partners, leading to a strong foundation of trust, support, and effective communication in their relationships.

An increased need for security and closeness, frequently accompanied by fears of abandonment, are characteristics of anxious-preoccupied attachment. People with this style may become overly preoccupied with their relationships, experience intense emotions, and seek constant validation from their partners.

Dismissive-avoidant attachment is characterized by a desire for independence and self-sufficiency. Individuals with this style tend to downplay the significance of close relationships and may struggle with emotional intimacy. They often prefer to deal with problems on their own and may appear distant or detached.

Fearful-avoidant (disorganized) attachment combines elements of both anxious and avoidant styles. People with this style exhibit conflicting desires for closeness and independence, leading to a cycle of approaching and then distancing themselves from their partners. They might experience inner turmoil and uncertainty about their relationships.

Understanding our attachment style is essential for unraveling patterns of behavior and emotional responses that arise within our relationships. By delving into our childhood experiences, we gain insights into the origins of relationship anxieties, insecurities, and tendencies toward overthinking. This exploration is not about blaming caregivers but about recognizing how early experiences have shaped our perceptions and behaviors.

Healing and personal growth can stem from acknowledging and addressing these past wounds. With this awareness, individuals can work towards developing a more secure attachment style, fostering healthier relationships in adulthood. Therapy and self-reflection are valuable tools for processing these early experiences, fostering self-awareness, and ultimately enhancing the quality of our intimate connections. Through introspection and effort, individuals can reshape their attachment narratives and embark on a journey of building more fulfilling and satisfying relationships.

How Past Relationships Shape Present Behavior

The tapestry of our past romantic relationships is woven with threads of emotion, experience, and memory, leaving an indelible mark on the canvas of our psyche. Every heartbreak, betrayal, or unmet need becomes a brushstroke, painting the landscape of our emotional landscape and shaping the lens through which we view our current partnerships. The echoes of these experiences reverberate within us, sculpting the contours of our approach and navigation in the realm of love.

Heartbreak, that universal human ache, can become a silent architect of our behavior. The scars it leaves are not just skin-deep; they etch themselves into our emotional core, rendering us cautious or guarded. The memory of vulnerability and betrayal can erect walls, prompting us to approach new relationships with trepidation, fearing that opening up might invite pain.

Betrayal, another formidable specter, casts its shadow on the canvas of trust. The echoes of broken promises and shattered faith can ripple through time, leaving us wary and suspicious. The innocence of believing in someone unconditionally can morph into skepticism, making it a challenge to fully entrust our hearts to another.

Unmet emotional needs, like seeds left untended, can grow into a tangle of vines that weave their way into our interactions. If we have felt neglected or unsupported in the past, we might find ourselves yearning for validation and assurance in our present relationships. Conversely, we might become overly dependent on our partners, seeking from them what was missing in our past connections.

Our current behavior is impacted by the dynamics of our previous relationships. The fear of being misunderstood or rejected can influence the way we communicate, causing us to hide our true thoughts and feelings. Emotional responses become nuanced by the ghosts of the past; an innocent comment might trigger a disproportionate reaction borne from previous wounds.

However, by acknowledging the threads that connect past and present relationships, a path to liberation emerges. We become archaeologists of our own emotional histories, excavating buried patterns and dynamics. This newfound self-awareness is a lantern guiding us out of the labyrinth of unhealthy patterns, illuminating the avenues that lead to more positive interactions with our partners.

Healing from past relationship wounds is an alchemical process that transforms pain into growth.

The journey towards breaking free from the chains of old wounds involves tending to the wounds with compassion, unpacking the baggage with introspection, and reframing the narrative with self-empowerment. This healing is the cornerstone for fostering the trust and intimacy required for nurturing healthy connections in the present. As we mend the bridges that have been burned and mend the wounds that have been left open, we pave the way for a new tapestry of love, one where the colors of resilience, understanding, and compassion are interwoven.

Each step we take toward healing is a step closer to rewriting our relationship story, forging connections that are based not on the scars of the past but on the potential for a brighter, more harmonious future.

Addressing Unresolved Emotional Baggage

The human heart is a complex vessel, capable of harboring both the sweet nectar of love and the bitter residues of pain. Unresolved emotional baggage from our past can be like an anchor, weighing down our present relationships and impeding their progress. The feelings of hurt, anger, or abandonment that we carry can cast a long shadow, distorting our perceptions and triggering a cascade of reactions that reverberate far beyond their origins.

These unresolved emotions have a way of infiltrating our interactions like silent infiltrators, distorting our communication, and eroding our sense of security. The scars of past wounds left unattended might manifest as relationship anxiety and overthinking, sowing seeds of doubt and suspicion where trust should flourish. Our minds become haunted landscapes, where every innocent action can be interpreted as a hidden agenda and every moment of silence can be amplified into a symphony of negative assumptions.

Emotional intimacy— that delicate dance of vulnerability and connection— becomes challenging when we're shackled by unresolved emotional baggage. The fear of being hurt again might lead us to withhold our true selves, choosing instead to don masks that shield us from potential pain. These barriers may prevent us from fully opening up to our partners, trapping us in a cycle of emotional distance that stifles the growth of our relationships.

Acknowledging and processing this emotional baggage becomes a crucial step toward liberation.

Self-reflection is the compass that guides us through the labyrinth of our emotions, allowing us to excavate buried pain and examine its roots. With each layer we uncover, we gain insight into how these wounds have shaped our perceptions and influenced our behavior. This understanding doesn't absolve the past, but it grants us the power to rewrite our present and future.

Professional support can serve as a guiding light on this journey of healing. Therapists offer a safe space for exploration where the tangled threads of our emotional history can be unraveled and rewoven. Their guidance equips us with the tools to process our feelings, challenge distorted beliefs, and reframe our narrative in ways that foster growth and emotional freedom.

Forgiveness, an essential alchemical ingredient, helps us transmute pain into growth. Forgiving ourselves for mistakes made and forgiving others for their shortcomings liberates us from the shackles of resentment. This act of grace creates space for new connections and fresh beginnings, enabling us to approach relationships with an open heart and a willingness to embrace vulnerability.

As we shed the weight of unresolved emotional baggage, our relationships become fertile ground for transformation. The walls that once stood as barriers crumble, allowing intimacy to flourish. With each layer of healing, we forge deeper connections, built not on the remnants of the past but on the potential for a harmonious and enriching future. By taking these steps towards healing, we embark on a journey of liberation, creating a legacy of healthier connections and nurturing a garden of love that blossoms with authenticity and trust.

The Role of Self-Compassion in Healing

Embarking on a journey through the corridors of our past is a delicate endeavor, one that requires us to navigate the labyrinth of memories and emotions with gentle hands and a compassionate heart. As we delve into the recesses of our history, it's paramount to remember that this process isn't about reopening wounds but about tending to them with the tenderness they deserve. Approaching this expedition with self-compassion is the compass that guides us through the complexities of confronting our past pain and trauma.

Reflection can be like peering into a mirror that reflects not just the image of our experiences but also the emotions embedded within them. It's natural to feel a swirl of emotions during this exploration—sadness, anger, and fear—and it's equally natural to feel vulnerable in the face of these emotions. Self-compassion serves as the soft cushion that supports us as we navigate this terrain, reminding us that it's okay to feel, to hurt, and to heal.

Imagine extending to yourself the same comforting words and gestures you would offer to a dear friend in distress. Self-compassion isn't about erasing the pain but about holding space for it and acknowledging its presence without judgment. It's about offering yourself a hand to hold in moments of darkness and whispering words of kindness to the wounded parts of your soul.

Cultivating self-compassion creates an inner sanctuary, a haven of understanding where healing and growth can flourish. Just as a gardener tends to fragile seeds with care, you nurture your emotional landscape with tenderness.

This practice creates an environment that counteracts the harsh winds of self-blame, the storms of shame, and the chill of judgment. Instead, self-compassion becomes the warm sun that encourages the sprouting of self-acceptance and understanding.

Breaking free from the chains of self-blame and shame is a liberation of the spirit. When we wrap ourselves in the embrace of self-compassion, we learn to view our past experiences not as marks of failure but as chapters of our personal narrative. We release the burdens of perfectionism and embrace our humanity, acknowledging that pain is part of the human experience. With self-compassion, we don't shy away from confronting our past; we meet it with open arms, ready to learn, heal, and grow.

As we tread the path of self-compassion, we become architects of our own emotional landscape. We lay the foundation for understanding and acceptance, creating a space where the wounds of the past can be tended to with care and tenderness. Through this practice, we emerge from the shadows of self-criticism and judgment into the light of self-love and healing. With each step, we forge a path toward a richer, more compassionate relationship with ourselves and, ultimately, with the world around us.

Embracing the Present Moment

In our quest for healing and growth, we journey not only through the corridors of the past but also across the landscapes of the present. As we delve into the depths of our past experiences, it's important to remember that our current relationships exist in the here and now, requiring our full presence and attention.

This delicate balance between honoring our history and embracing the present moment is where mindfulness steps in as our guiding lantern.

Imagine life as a tapestry woven with threads of time— past, present, and future. While it's valuable to examine the intricate patterns of the past threads, fixating solely on them can cast shadows on the vibrant colors of the present and the potential of the future. Likewise, excessive worrying about what might come can blur the beauty of what's unfolding before us. Mindfulness is the loom that helps us weave these threads together, creating a harmonious whole.

At its essence, mindfulness involves being present with an open heart, fully attuned to the thoughts, feelings, and sensations that arise within us. It's about engaging in the present moment without judgment or preconceived notions, allowing experiences to unfold naturally. When it comes to relationships, mindfulness encourages us to approach each interaction with open hearts and minds, free from the burden of the past's wrongs or the uncertainty of the future.

Cultivating mindfulness offers us a sanctuary of clarity amid the chaos of emotions. By observing our thoughts and feelings from a more objective standpoint, we gain distance from the grip of relationship anxiety and overthinking. Rather than becoming entangled in the web of our emotions, we become observers of them, witnessing their ebb and flow without becoming consumed.

With heightened awareness, we respond to relationship challenges from a place of emotional balance. By giving us the ability to pause before acting, mindfulness enables us to select reactions that are guided by our intentions and values rather than being solely by impulsive emotions. This mindful space provides room for meaningful conversations, deeper understanding, and genuine connection.

Just as a skilled gardener tends to their garden with care, nurturing each bud and tending to each leaf, mindfulness nurtures the garden of our relationships. It helps us clear away the weeds of assumption, prune the branches of overthinking, and water the seeds of authentic connection.

Through mindfulness, we create a space where our relationships can blossom, grounded in the richness of the present moment.

In this dance between past, present, and future, mindfulness becomes our partner, guiding us with gentle steps. It teaches us that while the past shapes us and the future calls to us, the only moment we truly possess is the present. By anchoring ourselves in this moment, we enrich our connections with partners, nurturing relationships that thrive on the fertile soil of mindful awareness.

Breaking the Cycle of Self-Fulfilling Prophecies

Our thoughts and beliefs can occasionally become self-fulfilling prophecies in the context of relationships. For instance, if we routinely expect rejection or the worst-case scenario, our actions might unintentionally result in the very situations we fear. In this section, we delve into the dynamics of self-fulfilling prophecies and how they contribute to relationship anxiety and overthinking.

By becoming aware of our thought patterns and challenging negative beliefs, we can interrupt the cycle of self-fulfilling prophecies. This empowers us to respond to our partners and situations in ways that promote trust, openness, and emotional intimacy, fostering more positive and fulfilling connections.

Chapter Three: Identifying Triggers and Patterns

Identifying Triggers and Patterns

In this chapter, we shift our focus toward recognizing the triggers and patterns that fuel relationship anxiety and overthinking. Identifying these key elements is crucial for gaining insight into our emotional responses and thought processes. By shining a light on our triggers and patterns, we lay the groundwork for breaking free from the grip of anxiety and cultivating healthier ways of relating to ourselves and others.

Recognizing Common Triggers for Anxiety and Overthinking

Life is a tapestry woven with threads of experiences, each thread holding the potential to evoke emotions that can propel us toward love or plunge us into anxiety and overthinking. Triggers, those delicate keys that unlock the chambers of our emotional responses, play a significant role in this intricate dance. These triggers are like chords struck on the strings of our hearts, resonating with the memories and wounds we've amassed along our journey.

Jealousy, a common trigger, is like a whisper of doubt that can grow into a roaring storm. It arises when we perceive a threat to a valued relationship, casting shadows of insecurity over our sense of self-worth. The fear of losing what we hold dear can send ripples of anxiety through our emotional landscape, causing us to question our partner's intentions and actions.

Uncertainty about a partner's feelings, another delicate chord, can awaken echoes of past hurts. Those who have experienced rejection or emotional neglect might find themselves entangled in a web of doubt. Small gestures or words can become magnified, dissected for hidden meanings, and analyzed for hidden intentions, spiraling into overthinking that clouds the clarity of our interactions.

Past experiences, like buried treasures, can be triggers that send shockwaves through our emotions. A careless word or an innocent action can awaken dormant memories, rekindling old wounds and resurrecting the pain we thought we had buried. These triggers cast a shadow on the present, making it challenging to fully engage with our partners without the specter of the past hovering nearby.

However, in recognizing these triggers lies our power to reshape our emotional landscape. Awareness acts as a shield, allowing us to anticipate and navigate challenging situations with greater poise. When we identify our triggers, we become architects of our emotional responses, no longer at the mercy of automatic reactions. This recognition empowers us to take conscious steps toward reducing their impact.

Managing triggers involves a two-fold dance. The first step is self-awareness – recognizing the sensations, thoughts, and emotions that arise when a trigger is activated. By acknowledging these reactions without judgment, we defuse their power to hijack our responses. The second step is proactive response – taking deliberate actions to address triggers before they escalate. This might involve communication with our partners, seeking support from friends or professionals, or practicing self-care techniques to soothe heightened emotions.

Through this dance, we cultivate emotional resilience. Instead of being swept away by the currents of anxiety and overthinking, we learn to navigate the waters with steady hands and a clear mind. Triggers lose their potency as we embrace a deeper understanding of ourselves and our emotional landscape.

In the symphony of relationships, triggers are the unexpected notes that can either create discord or add depth. By acknowledging and addressing them, we compose a melody of understanding and growth. As we learn to master the chords of our triggers, we create harmonious connections that resonate with authenticity, compassion, and emotional balance.

Unraveling Harmful Relationship Patterns

Relationships often follow distinct patterns based on our past experiences and attachment styles. Some of these patterns may be beneficial, fostering trust and intimacy, while others can be harmful, perpetuating relationship anxiety and overthinking. In this section, we delve into the various relationship patterns and identify those that contribute to our emotional distress.

Whether it's a pattern of constant reassurance-seeking, withdrawing emotionally when faced with vulnerability, or adopting a critical stance towards our partners, we examine the dynamics at play. Understanding these patterns allows us to challenge and transform the ones that hinder our personal growth and the growth of our relationships.

Tracking and Analyzing Your Thoughts and Reactions

Our thoughts and reactions play a significant role in how we perceive and engage with our relationships. In this section, we explore techniques for tracking and analyzing our thoughts and emotional responses. Journaling, mindfulness practices, and self-reflection exercises can be valuable tools for gaining clarity on the thought patterns that contribute to relationship anxiety and overthinking.

By engaging in these practices, we develop a deeper understanding of the underlying beliefs and assumptions that drive our emotional responses. Armed with this knowledge, we can challenge irrational thoughts, reframe negative beliefs, and replace destructive patterns with healthier alternatives.

This chapter has provided us with a comprehensive exploration of triggers and patterns that underlie relationship anxiety and overthinking. By recognizing our triggers, unraveling harmful relationship patterns, and tracking our thoughts and reactions, we gain valuable insights into the root causes of our emotional distress.

Awareness is the first step towards change, and as we continue to deepen our self-awareness, we become better equipped to navigate our relationships with greater clarity and emotional balance. In the following chapters, we will delve into practical techniques and strategies to manage anxiety and overthinking effectively. Embrace the knowledge gained in this chapter, and let us move forward with confidence on our journey toward overcoming relationship anxiety and overthinking.

Chapter Four: Cultivating Self-Awareness and Mindfulness

We turn our attention in this Chapter to the potent techniques of self-awareness and mindfulness. The foundation for overcoming relationship anxiety and overthinking is these techniques. We gain a deeper understanding of our emotions, triggers, and mental patterns by practicing self-awareness. Contrarily, mindfulness enables us to be present in our interactions and respond to difficulties with more clarity and compassion.

Adopting Mindfulness Techniques for Contentment

Mindfulness is the soft whisper that draws us to the sanctuary of the present moment in the tumult of existence. It's an invitation to remove ourselves from the confusion and to live fully in the now, free from the constraints of the past or the uncertainties of the future. We set out on a transforming trip in this part to comprehend the tremendous significance of adopting mindfulness practices—a journey that grounds us, centers us, and nourishes the very core of our relationships.

Principles of Mindfulness

Being mindfully present in every moment and allowing us to experience life as it is is the art of being. We observe our thoughts and feelings in this state of awareness without attachment or judgment. The goal of mindfulness is to gently direct our attention back to the present while acknowledging our thoughts rather than deleting them.

The Doorway to Stillness is meditation.

The cornerstone of mindfulness is meditation, a technique that helps us reach our innermost selves. It is an internal trip that takes us deep inside our awareness. We can learn to still our minds and hear the cries of our souls through meditation. In the middle of the tumultuous symphony of life, it is a moment of silence that brings tremendous clarity and peace.

Exercises for Deep Breathing: The Dance of Breath and Being

Deep breathing exercises are the dance that takes place on our breath, which serves as a bridge between the mind and the body. When we breathe mindfully, we concentrate on each breath's smooth rise and fall. It's a technique that grounds us in the here and now, quiets our chattering minds, and ties us to life's rhythm.

Body Scanning: The Internal Journey

Body scanning is a technique that encourages us to mentally travel across the geography of our bodies. We go through this environment mindfully, recognizing each sensation and letting go of tension. It's an effective tool to help us stay in the now and let go of worry and overthinking.

Encouragement of Emotional Resilience

Emotional resilience is a product of mindfulness. We can notice our emotions objectively by practicing mindfulness. We notice them and let them move in and out like ocean waves. This distance promotes resilience, allowing us to respond to difficulties with composure and comprehension.

As we adopt mindfulness techniques, we enter the world of mindful living. It's a way that opens up a haven of serenity within of us that radiates peace and comprehension into our interpersonal interactions. Every connection becomes a fascinating and enlightening experience thanks to mindfulness, which serves as a bridge between us and the people we love and our true selves.

Recognizing the Strength of Self-Awareness

Self-awareness serves as the cornerstone for developing enduring connections. It is the profound art of looking inward and penetrating the layers of our brain to see the complex interactions between our thoughts, feelings, and actions. This introspective journey has enormous value in the world of relationships because it enables us to manage the challenges of human connection with clarity and wisdom.

Self-awareness is fundamentally the conscious recognition and understanding of our emotional world. To comprehend the peaks and valleys of our emotions, the complex web of our thoughts, and the motivations guiding our behavior, we go deep within our psyche. This process represents a profound understanding—a sincere attempt to understand the what and why of who we are—rather than merely a passing acknowledgment.

Self-awareness proves to be a powerful friend in the fight against relationship anxiety and overthinking. Anxiety frequently results from unresolved problems, traumas from the past, or worries about the future. We begin to understand these fundamental causes through self-reflection. We recognize the thinking and behavior patterns that feed our fears, which enables us to face them head-on.

We can reframe our viewpoints and modify our behaviors by comprehending the causes of our concerns and propensity for overthinking. This newly acquired knowledge gives us the ability to control our emotional responses in the context of interpersonal relationships. We may actively decide how we react to difficult circumstances rather than letting fear or anxiety dictate our actions.

Additionally, self-awareness enables us to express our demands and worries in more effective ways. We may communicate with our partners in a helpful and empathic way when we are aware of our emotional triggers and sensitivities. Open communication creates a path to understanding and increases connection and empathy in a relationship.

self-awareness empowers us to foster stronger relationships by encouraging empathy, understanding, and deliberate action. It's a journey of empowerment and growth where we become more true versions of ourselves, able to create deep connections based on love, trust, and understanding.

Communication that is mindful in relationships

Healthy relationships are built on effective communication. Being present, focused, and compassionate when speaking with others is part of mindful communication. We examine the foundations of mindful communication and how it might improve our interactions in this part.

We foster frank and open communication by engaging in active listening and speaking with sincerity and empathy. By navigating disagreements with empathy and respect, mindful communication helps us avoid misconceptions and promotes a closer relationship with our relationships.

highlighting how self-awareness and mindfulness can help people overcome relationship anxiety and overthinking. Adopting mindfulness techniques helps us stay in the present, which reduces our reactivity and emotional distress. Insights into our triggers and patterns are revealed through self-awareness, which opens the door to making deliberate and healthy relationship decisions.

We develop our emotional resiliency and our relationships with ourselves and our partners as we keep up these practices. The ways to properly manage stress and anxiety will be covered in more detail in the next chapters. Let us continue on our path of growth and healing with fresh confidence and compassion as our allies, using self-awareness and mindfulness as our guides.

Chapter Five: Rewiring Negative Thought Patterns

In this Chapter, we delve into the power of rewiring negative thought patterns. Our thoughts greatly influence our emotions and behaviors, and negative thought patterns can fuel relationship anxiety and overthinking. By challenging and transforming these patterns, we gain the ability to approach our relationships with greater positivity, openness, and self-compassion. This chapter explores practical techniques to reframe our thinking and cultivate healthier perspectives.

Challenging Negative Self-Talk in Relationships

Within the recesses of our minds lies a powerful force—a relentless internal dialogue that can shape our perception of self and the world around us. This dialogue, known as negative self-talk, is an insidious stream of self-criticism, doubt, and self-blame that weaves its way through our consciousness. Its effects are far-reaching, seeping into the very foundations of our self-esteem and confidence. When it comes to relationships, negative self-talk emerges as a formidable adversary, capable of fomenting anxiety and overthinking.

This toxic internal chatter has the ability to erode our sense of self-worth, leading to a ripple effect of doubt that permeates our interactions with others.

It whispers tales of inadequacy, magnifying perceived flaws and past mistakes. As we succumb to these negative narratives, they cast shadows of doubt upon our ability to be loved and accepted by those we hold dear.

In the realm of relationships, negative self-talk can manifest in various forms. Catastrophizing, a common negative thought pattern, finds us expecting the worst possible outcomes, assuming that a minor disagreement will escalate into a relationship-ending catastrophe. Mind-reading, another detrimental pattern, convinces us that we know what others are thinking—usually assuming the worst—and can be a potent source of anxiety.

The impact of such negative narratives on our emotional well-being cannot be overstated. Relationship anxiety and overthinking often find their roots in this relentless self-criticism. It breeds insecurities and fuels a perpetual state of worry, creating a cycle that hinders our ability to engage authentically and openly in our relationships.

However, it's not a battle lost. Through the application of cognitive restructuring techniques, we can challenge and reframe this damaging inner dialogue. Cognitive restructuring encourages us to dissect these negative thoughts, examining their validity and replacing them with more balanced, compassionate alternatives.

By fostering a kinder and more supportive inner dialogue, we cultivate emotional resilience and self-acceptance. We nurture an environment within ourselves that fosters growth, understanding, and a genuine sense of worthiness. This newfound self-compassion becomes the bedrock upon which we build healthier relationships, unshackled from the chains of anxiety and overthinking.

Through the transformative power of cognitive restructuring, we embark on a journey toward healing and growth—a journey that liberates us from the clutches of negative self-talk, allowing us to forge meaningful and enriching connections with others.

Replacing Catastrophic Thinking with Realistic Perspectives

In the intricate tapestry of our thoughts, catastrophic thinking emerges as a tangled thread, capable of distorting our perceptions and triggering unwarranted distress. It's the art of envisioning the worst outcomes in vivid detail, painting a canvas of dread and anxiety within our minds. This habitual way of thinking, if left unchecked, can cast a pervasive shadow over our relationships and overall well-being.

In the realm of relationships, the repercussions of catastrophic thinking are far-reaching. It infuses a dose of negativity into our interactions, clouding our judgment and influencing our behavior. Each minor disagreement or hiccup is blown out of proportion, with our minds conjuring catastrophic scenarios where love is lost, friendships shattered, and bonds irreparably broken.

This heightened anxiety can be paralyzing, preventing us from fully engaging with our loved ones. We become ensnared in a web of "what-ifs" and worst-case scenarios, leaving us emotionally exhausted and disconnected from the present moment.

However, there's a beacon of hope—the transformative power of cognitive reframing. Through conscious effort and practice, we can identify and challenge these catastrophic thoughts. We learn to pause, step back from the whirlwind of anxious thoughts, and objectively assess the situation.

Cognitive reframing encourages us to replace these destructive thoughts with more realistic and balanced perspectives. We ask ourselves: Is the situation truly as dire as we imagine? Are there alternative explanations or outcomes that we might be overlooking?

This shift in perspective is akin to cleansing a foggy lens. Suddenly, the overwhelming panic begins to subside, making room for clarity and rationale.

We gain the ability to respond to challenges in our relationships with a calmer demeanor and a more measured approach.

By embracing this approach, we liberate ourselves from the clutches of catastrophic thinking, fostering resilience and a newfound sense of control over our anxious thoughts. Relationships, once shrouded in anxiety, become an arena where we can navigate with grace and understanding.

The path to emotional freedom lies in our ability to transform catastrophic thinking into realistic perspectives. It's a journey toward inner peace and stronger connections, where the mind is no longer a prisoner of exaggerated fears but a willing participant in the art of healthy, thriving relationships.

Empowering the Mind: Developing Positive Affirmations

In the realm of our psyche, where thoughts hold immeasurable power, positive affirmations emerge as beacons of light, capable of dispelling the shadows of negativity. They are declarations of self-belief, confidence, and love that reverberate through our consciousness, challenging the discordant tunes of self-doubt. Through their transformative influence, we pave a path toward heightened self-esteem and resilience.

In the intricate dance between our thoughts and emotions, negative thought patterns can often dominate, leaving us mired in self-criticism and doubt. This is where positive affirmations step in as warriors of change. They act as a counterforce, challenging the destructive narratives that have taken root within our minds.

In the sphere of relationships, their role is profound. Relationship anxiety and overthinking find their roots in these negative narratives, in the belief that we are somehow unworthy of love or acceptance. Positive affirmations dismantle these beliefs, brick by brick, until we stand on a solid foundation of self-assurance.

Developing personalized affirmations is an art in itself. It involves crafting statements that resonate deeply with our values, goals, and aspirations. These affirmations are not mere words; they are reflections of our true selves, encapsulating the essence of who we strive to be.

By incorporating these positive affirmations into our daily routine, we orchestrate a symphony of positivity within our minds. We replace the harsh, discordant notes of self-critique with a melody of self-love and empowerment. As we consistently affirm our strengths and worth, the rhythm of our thoughts changes, reinforcing healthier patterns and nurturing a profound sense of empowerment.

This transformation isn't a one-time event but a continuous journey. With each affirmation uttered, we are reminding ourselves of our inherent worth, our unique capabilities, and the boundless potential that resides within us. With time and dedication, these affirmations become an integral part of our psyche, influencing our actions and reactions in relationships.

In essence, positive affirmations offer us a lifeline—a way to pull ourselves from the depths of self-doubt and anxiety. They are the seeds of self-belief we plant, nurturing a forest of confidence that shields us against the storms of negativity. Through the gentle power of positive affirmations, we embark on a transformative journey toward self-acceptance and thriving relationships.

This Chapter highlights the importance of rewiring negative thought patterns to overcome relationship anxiety and overthinking. By challenging negative self-talk, replacing catastrophic thinking with realistic perspectives, and developing positive affirmations, we take proactive steps to transform our thinking and foster emotional well-being.

As we continue to practice these techniques, we strengthen our mental resilience and cultivate a more positive and compassionate mindset. In the upcoming chapters, we will explore techniques to manage stress and anxiety effectively, fostering healthier and more fulfilling relationships. Armed with these tools to reframe our thinking, let us move forward with greater confidence and optimism on our journey of growth and healing.

Chapter Six: Managing Stress and Anxiety

This chapter focuses on helpful methods for managing stress and anxiety. Stress and anxiety can have a negative impact on our emotional health and social connections, as well as on overthinking and relationship anxiety. We empower ourselves to navigate difficult situations with increased resilience and maintain emotional equilibrium in our relationships by establishing coping methods and relaxation techniques.

Stress Management Methods

Stress frequently acts as an unwanted crescendo in the fast-paced symphony of life, upsetting the harmony of our well-being. It is an unavoidable travel companion, but when it overflows, its discordant notes can echo through our mental and physical domains, leaving a path of fatigue and imbalance in its wake. In this section, we'll look at a variety of stress-reduction strategies that can help to calm the chaos of overwhelm and promote inner harmony.

Exercises for Deep Breathing

Deep breathing exercises ebb and flow, grounding us in the present moment like the constant cadence of the ocean waves. The anxious melodies within can be altered by the simple act of taking a deep breath in and letting it fill our lungs before expelling and letting go of the tensions that bind us. Deep breathing acts as a passageway to serenity and a reminder that we have the ability to restore our sense of peace with each breath.

progressively relaxing the muscles

Progressive muscle relaxation encourages us to be still in the midst of commotion, to go within, and to intentionally release the tension that frequently builds up in our muscles. Each muscle group has a turn to relax and release tension as we are lead on a trip through our bodies. We discover ourselves being engulfed by a calming song of peace and physical ease as the tension fades.

Directed Imagery

Similar to a musical composition, guided imagery enables us to create in-depth mental pictures of peaceful places. It's an invitation to explore the imaginary countries of our minds and lose ourselves in a tranquil, serene environment. Stress releases its hold as we imagine and design this inner beauty, and we find comfort in the harmony we have created.

We build a wall against stress by implementing these stress-reduction techniques into our daily lives. They develop into our resiliency tools, bringing a quieter frequency to our hearts and brains. The discord of stress is transformed into the pleasant symphony of inner calm when we practice a state of contentment and serenity.

This internal harmony manifests as an outward elegance in the world of relationships. We are able to respond to our loved ones with compassion, meet problems with a steadier gaze, and move gracefully through emotional ebbs. Because of our newfound peace, the relationships we value most are no longer drowned out by the din of stress but instead stand strong in the face of the storm.

Techniques for reducing stress provide us an opportunity to create a symphony of tranquility amidst the chaos of life. We discover the art of thriving, not just surviving, in the ever-evolving song of existence through their practice.

Coping strategies for anxiety attacks

Finding a lifeboat can mean the difference between being carried away by the waves and gaining stable ground in the stormy sea of anxiety episodes. Similar to an unexpected storm, anxiety can sweep us up and leave us unable to escape its never-ending chaos. In this section, we look at a variety of coping skills that act as our compass, directing us away from the turbulent waves of worry and towards calming shores.

Exercises for Grounding

Grounding exercises are like the anchor that keeps us stable in the midst of the tempest when anxiety stirs up an internal storm. They reacquaint us with the present and firmly establish us in the here and now. Techniques like the 5-4-3-2-1 grounding exercise, which involves focusing on the five things we can see, four of the things we can touch, three of the things we can hear, two of the things we can smell, and one of the things we can taste, assist to anchor us in the moment and calm the whirlwind of anxiety.

Visualization

Visualization is like plotting a calm course through turbulent waters. It entails closing our eyes and imagining a calm, secure location—a quiet sanctuary to which we can flee when anxiety arises. This mental haven offers comfort and a momentary break from the storm, whether it's a sun-kissed beach, a beautiful forest, or a cozy reading nook.

Thought-Stopping

Anxiety frequently results from our minds' constant churning of unfavorable thoughts. We can end this damaging loop by using the thought-stopping technique. We mentally yell "Stop!" or "Cancel!" whenever a bad notion pops into our heads. The flow of negativity is abruptly stopped, which gives us a brief window of opportunity to switch the negative idea to a neutral or good one.

We have the ability to respond to anxious moments with resiliency and confidence by building a toolkit of coping techniques. These coping mechanisms aren't simply tools for us; they're also harmonic instruments that reverberate across our relationships, promoting a greater sense of support and understanding.

Anxiety may have a big impact on relationships and frequently has an impact on how we connect with our loved ones. But if we have coping skills, we can handle these situations gracefully. We can close the comprehension gap with our spouses and get their support and empathy by communicating our demands and using coping mechanisms when anxiety attacks.

Anxiety coping strategies provide us with a lighthouse—a waypoint through the choppy waters of anxiety. With these resources at our disposal, we may steer a course of toughness and resilience not only for our own selves but also for the relationships we value. It's the skill of using anxiety as a springboard for development and closer relationships.

Implementing Relaxation Techniques in Daily Life

Finding peaceful moments in the midst of the chaos of modern life is like discovering an oasis in the desert. Our lives are a never-ending tornado of obligations, requirements, and expectations. However, there is a chance for profound rest and renewal amidst this hectic dance. In this section, we set out on an adventure to investigate several relaxation techniques that can meld into the fabric of our daily lives, giving us a break from the chaos and luring peace.

Consciousness Training

Mindfulness meditation is a symphony of quiet in the midst of the noise of everyday life. It serves as a call to pause and completely inhabit the current moment without passing judgment. We find a haven of serenity in the soft rhythm of our breath and the pleasures that delight our senses. We may get off the stress rollercoaster and re-establish our connection to inner peace by incorporating brief mindfulness meditation sessions into our daily schedule.

Yoga

Yoga is a gentle choreography that unifies our being. It is a dance of the body and mind. It invites us to a state of tranquility through a combination of postures, breathing techniques, and attentive awareness. Even a few yoga stretches throughout the day or a morning yoga program can be life-changing. It reduces muscle tension, centers our thinking, and fosters a sense of inner equilibrium.

Time Spent in Nature

Nature is a skilled painter, creating serene and lovely landscapes. Entering the embrace of nature is like receiving a tender touch on the soul. It's a call to be in the moment amid the rustle of the leaves, the aroma of the land, and the embrace of the wide heavens. Nature provides us with a haven of quiet and an opportunity to recharge, whether it's a stroll in the park, a hike through the woods or simply sitting by a body of water.

Taking Part in Hobbies

Our interests and pastimes open doors to delight and relaxation. We can escape the rigors of daily life and lose ourselves in moments of pure enjoyment and creative expression by partaking in hobbies that speak to our soul, whether it's gardening, reading a great book, painting, playing an instrument, or any other activity.

By making relaxation a priority and including these techniques in our everyday routines, we provide ourselves with opportunities for self-care and emotional refueling. This investment in our own health has an impact on how we engage with other people, enabling us to treat our relationships with the same amount of tenderness and care.

Our emotional state has a significant impact on the dynamics we share with those we care about in relationships. We are more present and understanding in our interactions when we are calm, collected, and refreshed. We pay closer attention when we listen, empathize more fully, and love more completely.

An homage to self-love, incorporating relaxation techniques into daily life is a recognition that we deserve to take breaks from the stresses of life and recharge. By intentionally taking care of ourselves, we not only improve our own lives but also the lives of the people who are important to us.

This chapter provides us with useful tools for successful stress and anxiety management. We increase our emotional resiliency and keep a sense of inner calm by putting stress-reduction tactics into practice, creating coping mechanisms for anxiety attacks, and incorporating relaxation techniques into our daily lives.

As we keep using these strategies, we improve our capacity to handle relationship difficulties with poise and dignity. We will look at ways to improve emotional closeness, restore trust, and foster healthy relationships in the chapters that follow. Let's continue on our path of relationship development and healing with more poise and confidence as we manage our tension and anxiety.

Chapter Seven: Building Trust and Security

Any wholesome and satisfying relationship is built on trust. Building trust and security in our relationships with others is a key topic in this chapter. Overanalyzing and relationship anxiety can weaken trust, making it difficult to build lasting relationships. We empower ourselves to develop stronger and more durable relationships by learning techniques to reestablish trust and foster a sense of security.

Rebuilding Trust Following a Betrayed

The frail thread of trust is present throughout the intricate web of human connections. It can appear as though the very foundation of our relationship is tearing apart when that thread is severed by betrayal. The essential confidence we have in our loved ones is destroyed when they betray us, whether it is through breaking a commitment, being unfaithful, or crossing boundaries. We set out on a trip through the challenging but transforming process of restoring trust following such a violation in this part.

Recognizing the Effects of Betrayal

The fallout from betrayal is a turbulent sea of feelings. The deceived struggles against a storm of hurt, rage, perplexity, and unbelief. Once trust is betrayed, the wounds are severe. These mental wounds need time, compassion, and understanding to heal; they do not do it immediately.

The Foundation of Communication

The foundation of communication is the key to reestablishing confidence. Understanding all sides' points of view requires an honest and open discourse. The betrayed must voice their hurt and worries, and the betrayer must pay attention and recognize the seriousness of their acts.

Integrity and Openness

On the path to reestablishing trust, honesty turns into a source of encouragement. The betrayer must be open and honest about their acts, reasons, and any precautions taken to avoid a repeat. By displaying a dedication to candor and openness, transparency aids in mending the trust gap.

Responsibility and Amendments

One essential stage in the healing process is accepting responsibility for the betrayal. The betrayer must be willing to make apologies and must be aware of the consequences of their conduct. This can entail modifying one's behavior, obtaining counseling, or taking any other necessary steps to reveal a true dedication to restoring trust.

Making a Healing Space Safe

Creating a supportive and safe atmosphere for healing requires active participation from both sides. This entails establishing boundaries, upholding them, and supporting one another as they travel the arduous road to recovery.

Rebuilding trust is a difficult process that needs commitment from both the betrayed party and the betrayer. It's a journey tainted by failures and uncertainties, but it's also one of resiliency and development. A stronger, more durable connection has the potential to develop as trust progressively grows again.

Relationships can become more resilient and powerful as a result of the loss and subsequent repair of trust. We turn the ashes of betrayal into the cornerstone of trust by being open with one another, being truthful with one another, and being genuinely committed to change. The scars are still there, but they serve as a reminder of how resilient people can be and how love has the strength to heal even the most serious wounds.

Transparency and Honesty in Communication

Any relationship depends on effective communication, which is a skill that must be learned for a bond to endure and grow. Open and honest communication is a vital brushstroke in this art. It serves as the blank canvas on which intimacy, trust, and understanding are painted. The fundamental importance of this type of communication in creating a solid, long-lasting connection with our partners is explored in this section.

Communicating Needs and Emotions

The capacity to express our sentiments and wants is at the heart of transparent and honest communication. This necessitates a thorough grasp of our own feelings as well as the bravery to bare them to our partners. It doesn't matter what the emotion is—joy, sorrow, impatience, or love—expressing it in a direct and kind way promotes empathy and understanding.

Increasing Comprehension and Trust

A sacred space is created by open conversation where both partners can express themselves without worrying about criticism or rejection. It's a bridge that crosses the miscommunication chasm and allows us to see the world from the perspective of our loved ones. The seeds of an enduring connection are nurtured when we pay attention to and comprehend one other's points of view.

Addressing Fears and Anxieties

Every relationship is susceptible to the effects of worries and fears. Transparent, honest communication serves as a light source in this dark place. It enables us to freely and productively confront these worries by bringing them to light. We expose our worries and insecurities to the enlightening light of awareness by talking about them, which lessens their ability to damage our relationship.

Increasing Emotional Bond

Genuine, emotional connections are characterized by open, unpretentious conversations. We cultivate a deep closeness that ties us together when we remove the layers and let our true selves be revealed. The intimacy that results from sharing our aspirations, dreams, concerns, and vulnerabilities with our partners deepens our connection on a spiritual level.

Open and honest communication is the golden thread in the fabric of a relationship, creating a pattern of love, understanding, and trust. It calls for effort, openness, and a desire to actually hear and be heard. This kind of communication has the power to change relationships and make them more durable when it is fostered and developed.

Let's accept honest, open communication as a necessary component in the chemistry of love. Let's talk honestly and compassionately because it is in the depths of our dialogues that the secret to a happy, lasting relationship lies—one in which love grows, trust grows, and understanding grows.

Setting Limits to Ensure a Secure Relationship

Boundaries act as the beautiful choreography that preserves balance and harmony in the complex dance of relationships. In any relationship, setting up good boundaries is essential to fostering a safe and loving environment, just to how a house's walls offer shelter and structure. In this section, we explore the deep importance of establishing and upholding boundaries in order to cultivate a strong and healthy relationship with our partners.

Recognizing the Range of Boundaries

In essence, boundaries are the lines we create to indicate our requirements, restrictions, and comfort zones in a relationship. These limits can appear in a variety of ways, including emotional, physical, and private ones. Physical, emotional, and personal boundaries all protect our privacy and emotional well-being. Personal boundaries outline our values, beliefs, and sense of self.

Boundaries' Function in Relationship Security

The sentinels that watch over a relationship's citadel are its boundaries. We establish a foundation of trust and respect for one another when we establish and uphold these boundaries. They serve as the unspoken agreements that set forth the rules of the union and create an atmosphere in which both parties feel free to be who they really are.

promoting trust and respect between people

Boundaries are the result of respect, which is the foundation of any relationship. We show a deep respect for each other's needs and limitations when we are honest about our boundaries and respect those of our partners. This shared respect serves as the cornerstone of trust, which is essential to a stable and enduring partnership.

Activating Genuine Engagement

Boundaries provide us the freedom to interact with others in a genuine and secure way. Our actual selves can come through when we recognize and express our boundaries. This sincerity not only improves the connection but also deepens our sense of identity and self-assurance.

We are establishing an environment where love and understanding can bloom by promoting a culture of respect for boundaries. It's a coordinated dance of empathy and compromise in which the partners respect and acknowledge each other's boundaries. Through this synchronized dance, we create a love story that is grounded on respect and understanding for one another and that endures the winds of discord.

Let's accept limits as the keepers of our hearts and the creators of solid and durable bonds. The key to a love that is both liberated and truly satisfying resides within the world of boundaries, so let us communicate them with love and honor them with grace.

Open lines of communication, understanding among parties, and a desire to overcome obstacles jointly all foster trust. Let's prioritize developing trust and security as necessary components in establishing the loving and supportive relationships we desire as we continue on our journey to overcoming relationship anxiety and overthinking.

Chapter Eight: Enhancing Emotional Intimacy

Intimacy on an emotional level is essential to every lasting relationship. The importance of emotional openness and vulnerability in overcoming relationship anxiety and overthinking is discussed in this chapter. Understanding the importance of emotional intimacy and looking into ways to improve it help us build stronger bonds with our partners and promote a sense of fulfillment and security in our relationships.

Vulnerability's Function in Relationships

For relationships to become meaningful and intimate, vulnerability is essential. Real connection and understanding can happen when we let our relationships see us at our most vulnerable. Here is a detailed explanation of how vulnerability functions in relationships:

Building Connection and Trust: The basis of trust is vulnerability. We demonstrate to our partners that we trust them with our most intimate thoughts and feelings when we open up and share our true selves—the good, the terrible, and the unknown. This act of trust encourages a stronger emotional bond, which makes the friendship more real and satisfying.

Emotional intimacy is the sharing of our innermost feelings, thoughts, and experiences. We express our worries, hopes, aspirations, and vulnerabilities when we are at our most open. Through this sharing, both parties can express themselves freely and without fear of rejection. It strengthens the relationship's emotional connection and increases the degree of closeness.

Promoting understanding and understanding: We invite our partners' understanding when we allow ourselves to be vulnerable. Since they are able to see us for who we really are, they are better able to comprehend our circumstances and feelings. When both partners are sensitive to one another's needs and feelings, a relationship becomes more compassionate and empathic.

Fostering Growth and Resilience: Being vulnerable entails recognizing our shortcomings and potential for improvement. Sharing these facets of who we are with our partners creates a space where we can develop as a couple. It aids in overcoming obstacles as a unit, boosting resilience and preserving the bond in the face of difficulty.

Overcoming Shame and Fear: Being vulnerable enables us to confront and get over our fear of being rejected or judged. It confronts the guilt associated with having flaws or imperfections. We challenge these unfavorable emotions and experiences when we are honest about our weaknesses, which results in a healthier self-image and a more optimistic perspective on the relationship.

Taking Down Barriers to Communication: People frequently hold back from speaking openly out of a sense of vulnerability. However, these communication obstacles are broken down through admitting vulnerability. Sincere discussions about our needs want, and feelings grow more natural, improving our comprehension of one another's viewpoints.

In order to keep our independence while recognizing interdependence within the partnership, vulnerability aids us in finding the right balance. It's about realizing that it's acceptable to rely emotionally on someone, and about letting them rely on us as well.

Building a Nurturing Environment: A relationship based on openness develops into a nurturing environment where partners encourage and support one another. It's a setting where we may be completely honest without fear, fostering an environment of love, acceptance, and development.

How to Improve Your Emotional Connection with Your Partner

Emotional intimacy is the musical note that resounds across the chambers of our hearts in the symphony of love. Building and nurturing emotional connection needs deliberate effort and attention, just as a musician practices constantly to hone their profession. We will examine practical methods in this section for enhancing our emotional ties with our spouses and creating a love song that endures through the centuries.

Having Meaningful Discussions

Conversations are the notes that make up a relationship's emotional song. We may navigate the depths of our emotions, concerns, hopes, and aspirations when we have deep, heartfelt dialogues with our partners. It entails actually hearing and comprehending each other's thoughts and feelings, not merely paying lip service to them. Weaving a tapestry of intimacy, we encourage the sharing of our most vulnerable selves by fostering a safe space for vulnerability.

Sharing Interests and Taking Part in Them

Our hearts synchronize to a rhythm created by shared interests. Finding interests or pastimes shared by both partners and participating in them together fosters a sense of community and closeness. It may involve making a new cuisine, going for a walk, creating art, or even watching a favorite TV program. Beautiful memories are made from these shared experiences, and they also promote a sense of community and connection.

Gratitude and Appreciation Expression

The mellow notes that reverberate throughout a relationship are gratitude and appreciation. A strong emotional bond is fostered when we take the time to express thanks for the little things, appreciate one another's efforts, and recognize the value the other person gives to our lives. These acts of thankfulness strengthen our relationship by serving as a reminder of our shared affection.

Active Listening and Empathy Training

The compass that leads us across the map of our partner's emotions is active listening. We demonstrate empathy and understanding when we sincerely listen, not just with our ears but also with our emotions. We can create trust and support by confirming our partner's emotions, validating their experiences, and being present throughout their happy or sad moments.

By committing to these tactics, we strengthen the emotional foundation of our partnership. Strong emotional ties foster a sense of stability and support, which reduces relationship anxiety and overthinking. The embrace gives us the reassurance that we are not traveling alone and that someone actually knows us and is there to support us as we go through the ups and downs of life.

Let's think of these tactics as the score to our emotional symphony. We develop a love that sings of comprehension, compassion, and enduring connection with every perfected note and chord—a love that reverberates through the ages, touching the very core of our being.

Creating Intimacy Through Active Listening and Empathy

Empathy and attentive listening are the delicate threads that weave the strongest relationships in the fabric of intimacy. They are the heart's inner whispers that carry great weight and create bonds that go beyond simple verbal exchanges. In this section, we'll examine the significant importance of being attentive and sympathetic to our partners' thoughts and feelings in order to foster a deep emotional closeness.

Active Listening: Its Vitality

In order to actively listen, we must fully engulf ourselves in the emotions and sensations being expressed. It entails giving our complete attention, maintaining eye contact, and demonstrating our presence and engagement nonverbally. We may create a space where our spouse feels truly valued and heard by putting aside outside distractions.

Empathy: The Link to Comprehension

Empathy is the capacity to put oneself in another person's position and experience their feelings. It serves as a bridge between our hearts, helping us to comprehend and respect their suffering. Not only do we deeply connect with the other person when we empathize, but we also acknowledge and share in their emotional journey. This potent demonstration of understanding encourages a sensation of being seen and understood, which is crucial for fostering emotional connection.

Empathy's Function in Validation

In a relationship, empathy is the currency of validation. It gives our partners comfort to know that their feelings and experiences are recognized and valued. When we react with empathy, we convey that their feelings are important and legitimate, establishing a secure environment for vulnerability. We may disclose our authentic selves without worrying about being judged because this validation serves as the cornerstone of intimacy and trust.

Building an Emotional Sharing Culture

We establish an environment where emotional sharing takes place in our connection when we continuously demonstrate empathy and active listening. When partners know they will be understood and cared for, they feel secure to communicate their thoughts and feelings in an open manner. Intimacy thrives in this setting of emotional openness, strengthening the threads that bind us together.

By practicing empathy and attentive listening, we show our partners that we value their emotional health. It's an opportunity to share their emotional world more honestly as well as a statement of our commitment to comprehending their wants and experiences. We cultivate a genuinely compassionate and profoundly intimate love through this true act of presence and understanding.

Let's see the great acts of love that empathy and active listening are. Let's listen to and feel what our partners are feeling with open hearts and ears. In this gentle dance of connection, we create a love that endures the test of time and is both heard and fully understood.

Emotional intimacy fosters a sense of security and trust, enabling us to handle relationship difficulties with more empathy and understanding. Let us prioritize emotional closeness as the foundation of our relationships as we continue on our path of growth and healing, generating greater fulfillment and joy in our connections with others.

Chapter Nine: Strengthening Your Relationship

In this chapter, we shift our focus to practical strategies for strengthening our relationships. Building a strong and healthy connection requires effort and dedication from both partners. By exploring conflict resolution skills, embracing compromise and flexibility, and practicing gratitude and appreciation, we foster a resilient and fulfilling relationship that can withstand the challenges of relationship anxiety and overthinking.

Conflict Resolution Skills for Lasting Connections

In the grand orchestra of relationships, conflict is the clash of cymbals, the dissonant notes that challenge the harmony. Yet, it is within the resolution of these conflicts that we find the true melody—a melody of understanding, growth, and lasting connection. In this section, we unravel the art and importance of effective conflict resolution skills, the conductor's baton that guides us to a harmonious symphony.

Active Listening

Conflict resolution begins with a humble act—listening. But not just any listening—active listening. It's the art of not only hearing the words but understanding the emotions and intentions behind them. When we truly listen, suspending judgment and offering empathy, we pave the path toward resolution. Our partner feels heard and acknowledged, which forms the bedrock of cooperation and understanding.

Assertive Communication

Assertive communication is the gentle yet firm brushstroke that paints a picture of our needs, feelings, and boundaries. It involves expressing our thoughts clearly, honestly, and respectfully, without being aggressive or passive. It allows us to convey our perspective, negotiate effectively, and find a middle ground where both parties' needs are acknowledged and respected.

Finding Common Ground

Conflict resolution is akin to a delicate dance where partners seek common ground. It's a process of collaboration, finding solutions that honor both perspectives. It involves recognizing the validity of each other's viewpoints and working together to create a compromise that bridges the gap and strengthens the bond.

Avoiding Harmful Communication Patterns

In the heat of conflict, harmful communication patterns can emerge—criticism, defensiveness, stonewalling, or contempt. These patterns exacerbate anxiety and overthinking, eroding the very foundation of trust. Recognizing and avoiding these destructive patterns is crucial for constructive conflict resolution. Instead, we strive for kindness, patience, and understanding in our dialogue.

Adopting these constructive conflict resolution strategies is a proactive step toward fostering a deeper emotional connection. It allows us to navigate disagreements with empathy and respect, creating an atmosphere of trust and security. When we learn to resolve conflicts in a healthy and constructive manner, we build a love that is not brittle but flexible, a love that can weather any storm.

let us wield the brush of effective conflict resolution with grace and precision. Let us engage in the dance of disagreement with an understanding heart and a willing spirit. For within the resolution of conflicts lies the promise of a love that grows stronger, more resilient, and more beautiful with each note of discord harmoniously resolved.

Nurturing Relationships through Compromise and Flexibility

In the intricate waltz of relationships, compromise and flexibility are the graceful steps that keep the dance flowing smoothly. It's the understanding that in a duet, both partners must adjust their steps to create a beautiful and harmonious performance. In this section, we celebrate the art of compromise and flexibility, recognizing their pivotal roles in creating a resilient and enduring connection.

The Essence of Compromise

Compromise is not a surrender; it's a thoughtful negotiation toward a middle ground. It's the recognition that both partners have needs and desires that deserve acknowledgment. By meeting each other halfway, we demonstrate our commitment to the relationship's well-being. Compromise is the bridge that connects our differences, allowing us to build a love that encompasses both.

Flexibility as a Virtue

Flexibility is the fluidity of our movements in the dance of love. It's the willingness to bend and adjust, to understand that change is a constant in any relationship. Being flexible with our expectations and behaviors allows us to adapt to evolving circumstances. Like a supple tree that withstands the storm, flexibility makes our relationships resilient, bending without breaking.

Seeking Win-Win Solutions

In the realm of compromise and flexibility, we seek not winners or losers, but solutions that uplift both partners. It's a mindset of abundance—a belief that there are options that can satisfy the needs and desires of both parties. When we strive for win-win solutions, we cultivate an atmosphere of cooperation and collaboration.

Reinforcing Emotional Intimacy

Compromise and flexibility reinforce the fabric of emotional intimacy. It's an acknowledgment that our partner's happiness and comfort are intertwined with our own. By demonstrating a willingness to accommodate and adjust, we send a powerful message of love and partnership. It's an act that nurtures a sense of togetherness, reinforcing our emotional connection.

By embracing compromise and flexibility, we create a love that is expansive and generous. It's a love that navigates the ebb and flow of life with grace and understanding. Through this dance of adaptability, our relationships evolve into something beautiful—a testament to our ability to embrace change and grow together.

let us celebrate the beauty of compromise and the grace of flexibility. Let us waltz through life hand in hand, adjusting our steps and finding a rhythm that is uniquely ours. For within the willingness to compromise lies the promise of a love that is enduring, resilient, and forever evolving.

Enriching Relationships through Gratitude and Appreciation

In the garden of relationships, gratitude and appreciation are the nurturing rays of sunlight that help love bloom and flourish. They are the simple yet profound gestures that water the roots of connection, allowing it to grow stronger and more vibrant. In this section, we immerse ourselves in the transformative power of gratitude and appreciation, recognizing their profound impact on the health and vitality of our relationships.

Acknowledging Our Partners' Contributions

Gratitude and appreciation are the mirrors that reflect our partners' efforts and contributions. They allow us to see and acknowledge the everyday acts of love and support that often go unnoticed. From the grand gestures to the small kindnesses, expressing gratitude for what our partners bring into our lives affirms their value and importance.

Fostering a Culture of Appreciation

Creating a culture of appreciation within our relationships is akin to tending to a garden. When we consistently express our thanks and admiration, we cultivate an environment where love and kindness can thrive. It's a cycle of giving and receiving; as we appreciate, we are appreciated in return, creating a positive feedback loop of affirmation and connection.

Deepening Emotional Connection

Gratitude and appreciation are the invisible threads that weave our hearts together. When we express our thankfulness, we not only acknowledge the actions but also the intention and love behind them. This fosters a deeper emotional connection, reinforcing our love and creating a sense of security within the relationship.

Resilience in the Face of Challenges

Gratitude and appreciation act as a shield, protecting our relationships during turbulent times. When we face challenges or conflicts, the reservoir of positive feelings built through gratitude helps us weather the storm. It's a reminder of the love and joy present in the relationship, grounding us and providing the strength to overcome hurdles.

By incorporating gratitude and appreciation into our relationship dynamics, we create a love that is rich and fulfilling. It's a love that thrives on the acknowledgment of efforts, the celebration of strengths, and the cherishing of the unique qualities our partners bring into our lives. Through this practice, we celebrate not only the 'big' moments but also the beautiful tapestry of 'small' moments that make up our shared journey.

let us embrace gratitude and appreciation as an essential part of our relationship repertoire. Let us water the garden of love with thankfulness and watch it bloom into a vibrant, flourishing oasis of connection. For within the language of gratitude lies the promise of a love that is enduring, appreciative, and endlessly beautiful.

This chapter highlights practical strategies for strengthening our relationships. By honing conflict resolution skills, embracing compromise and flexibility, and practicing gratitude and appreciation, we foster a supportive and fulfilling connection with our partners.

A strong and healthy relationship serves as a buffer against relationship anxiety and overthinking, providing us with a safe and nurturing space to grow and thrive. As we continue on our journey of growth and healing, let us prioritize strengthening our relationships, and cultivating love and trust that sustains us through life's ups and downs.

Chapter Ten: Seeking Professional Support and Growth

In this Chapter, we explore the importance of seeking professional help and personal growth in overcoming relationship anxiety and overthinking. While this book provides useful insights and practical techniques, there may be instances where professional guidance is beneficial. Additionally, personal growth and self-development are ongoing processes that enable us to build healthier and more fulfilling relationships.

Knowing When to Seek Counseling or Therapy

Relationships are like gardens, needing tender care, attention, and sometimes, the guidance of a seasoned gardener. Just as plants may need extra attention to flourish, relationships too can benefit from a little outside help at times. In this part, we're talking about knowing when it's a good idea to reach out for that extra support for your relationship.

When You Feel Stuck or Overwhelmed

Ever felt like you're in a maze with no way out? Relationships can feel that way too. If you find yourselves going in circles, feeling overwhelmed, or stuck in the same arguments, it's a good sign to reach out for help. A professional can be the map to guide you out of that maze.

During Big Life Changes

Life can throw big changes our way—moving to a new place, having a baby, or a loss in the family. These changes can rock the boat in a relationship. It's okay to seek help during these times to navigate the stormy waters together.

When Communication Hits a Roadblock

Communication is the heart of any relationship. When it starts to falter or feels like you're speaking different languages, it's a sign to consider counseling. A counselor can teach you new ways to talk and listen, ensuring you're on the same page.

If Trust is Shattered

Trust is like glass—once broken, it's hard to fix. If trust has been broken, seeking professional help is like the glue to put the pieces back together. A counselor can guide you on the path to rebuilding trust and healing.

If Intimacy Fades Away

Intimacy isn't just about physical closeness; it's about emotional connection too. If you feel a growing distance emotionally or physically, it's a good time to seek help. Professionals can assist in reigniting that spark and fostering a deeper bond.

When Mental Health is a Concern

Mental health matters! If either of you is struggling with mental health issues like anxiety or depression, it can affect the relationship. Seeking counseling helps both of you navigate these challenges together.

Seeking help isn't a sign of weakness. It's a brave step towards a stronger and healthier relationship. Just as you'd see a doctor for a physical ailment, a relationship counselor is the doctor for your relationship. They're there to listen, guide, and help your love garden bloom even more beautifully.

How to Choose the Right Relationship Expert

So you've decided it's time to bring in a helper, like a wise elder to guide your love story. But how do you find the right one? Let's break it down in simple words.

Ask for Recommendations

Just like you ask friends for restaurant recommendations, ask them about relationship helpers too! They might know someone awesome. People you trust can suggest a good match for you.

Check Online Directories

The internet is like a big library. Look up online directories for therapists. You can put in your location and what kind of help you need. It's like a dating app, but for finding the right therapist!

See Their Specialties

Therapists have different superpowers. Some are great at helping with couples, some with families, and some with individuals. Make sure to find one who's a superhero in the area you need help with.

Read Reviews and Ratings

It's like checking the ratings of a movie before watching it. Read what others say about the therapist. Did they find them helpful? It gives you a peek into what your experience might be.

Have a Chat First

Think of it like a coffee date. Many therapists offer a first chat for free. Take this chance to see if you vibe with them. Do you feel comfortable talking to them? Do they get what you're saying?

Trust Your Gut Feeling

Just like when you meet a new friend and you feel that click, trust your gut. If you feel good about a therapist, that's a green light!

Affordability Matters

Therapy is like a gym membership for your mind and heart. Check if they fit your budget. Some therapists offer sliding scales, which means they adjust the cost based on what you can pay.

The Benefits of Couples Therapy

In the grand tapestry of relationships, there are times when the threads of connection may fray, when the harmony may falter. It's during these times that finding the guidance of a skilled navigator—a couples therapist—can make all the difference. In this part, we unravel the numerous benefits of couples therapy, a sanctuary where love can be mended, strengthened, and rediscovered.

Safe Haven for Vulnerability

Couples therapy is a sanctuary—a haven where partners can be vulnerable, where they can peel back the layers and share their raw emotions. It's a neutral place, free from judgment and bias, where partners can explore their feelings, fears, and hopes in a safe and nurturing environment. Here, they find solace in knowing that their problems are heard and understood.

Understanding the Root Causes

Just as a gardener diagnoses the ailments of a plant, a skilled therapist helps couples find the root causes of their relationship challenges. These may be buried deep within, often adding to relationship anxiety and overthinking. Through insightful dialogue and guided introspection, couples can uncover these underlying problems, getting clarity and understanding.

Mastering the Art of Effective Communication

Communication is the cornerstone of any relationship, and couples therapy is the classroom where partners can learn this art. A therapist facilitates healthy dialogue, giving tools and techniques for successful communication. Partners learn to listen actively, express their thoughts clearly, and understand each other's views, leading to deeper connections and resolution of conflicts.

Developing Empathy and Understanding

Empathy is the bridge that links hearts, and couples therapy is the workshop where it can be built and fortified. With the therapist's help, partners learn to step into each other's shoes, to feel and understand the emotions and experiences of their beloved. This newfound empathy promotes a deeper understanding and compassion, bridging the emotional gaps that may have caused strife.

Rebuilding Trust and Emotional Intimacy

Trust and emotional intimacy, once fractured, can be rebuilt under the skilled direction of a therapist. Through therapeutic exercises and discussions, couples learn to mend the breaches in trust, building a foundation of security and openness. Emotional intimacy is rekindled, allowing partners to rediscover the profound link that first drew them together.

Couples therapy is a sacred place where relationships can be reborn, redefined, and rejuvenated. It's an investment in love, a testament to the pledge to navigate life's storms hand in hand. Through the gentle direction of a therapist, couples can rewrite their love story, creating a melody that resonates with understanding, compassion, and enduring connection.

let us welcome couples therapy as a transformative journey toward a love that endures. Let us shed our inhibitions and fears, for within the walls of therapy lies the promise of a relationship that thrives—a relationship that is resilient, understanding, and completely loving.

Individual Counseling for Personal Growth

In the grand tapestry of self-discovery and personal growth, individual counseling is the compass that leads us toward the road within. It's the beacon of light in the labyrinth of our thoughts, illuminating the corners where our fears, hopes, and dreams dwell. In this part, we unravel the transformative journey of getting individual counseling, a voyage that can reshape our relationship with ourselves and consequently, the world around us.

An Oasis of Personal Reflection

Individual counseling is the tranquil oasis in the desert of our lives—a place where we can pause, reflect, and delve into the depths of our being. It provides a safe and supportive environment where we can unravel our experiences, untangle our feelings, and make sense of our thought patterns. In this nurturing space, we find the roots of our anxieties and overthinking, illuminating the path toward healing and growth.

The Wisdom of Self-Understanding

In the realm of individual counseling, we start on a journey of self-exploration and self-understanding. Therapists, with their empathetic ears and professional understanding, guide us through the labyrinth of our thoughts. They help us unravel the threads of our past, understand the patterns of our present, and imagine the tapestry of our future. Through this understanding, we gain the wisdom to manage life's complexities with grace and resilience.

Cultivating Coping Strategies

Life often throws challenges our way, and individual counseling provides us with the tools to face them. Therapists help us develop coping strategies, providing us with an arsenal of skills to navigate worry, anxiety, and adversity. These tactics become the pillars of our emotional resilience, empowering us to face the world with a sense of calm and fortitude.

Enhancing Self-Awareness and Self-Compassion

Individual counseling is a mirror that reflects our true selves—a mirror that allows us to watch our strengths and flaws without judgment. Through this introspection, we gain a deeper knowledge of ourselves, nurturing self-awareness and self-compassion. As we learn to embrace our imperfections with kindness, we offer the same compassion to others, enriching our relationships with empathy and understanding.

By embracing individual counseling, we respect the journey of self-growth. It's an investment in ourselves, a pledge to unraveling the layers of our being, and a promise to bloom into our truest selves. Through this voyage, we not only transform our relationship with ourselves but also the way we connect to the world and those we cherish.

Embracing Lifelong Growth for a Fulfilling Journey

In the vast landscape of human life, personal growth is the evergreen forest, constantly flourishing, evolving, and beckoning us to wander deeper. It is a voyage without an end destination, a perpetual quest for self-improvement and enlightenment. In this section, we start on a trip to illuminate the profound significance of embracing lifelong growth—a journey that enriches not only ourselves but the very fabric of our relationships.

The Art of Continuous Self-Reflection

Personal growth is an art, and like any art form, it lives on contemplation and introspection. Continuous self-reflection is the brush that paints the surface of our lives. It's the conscious examination of our actions, thoughts, and beliefs—an introspective gaze that allows us to refine our strokes, creating a masterpiece of character and knowledge.

The Canvas of Learning and Adapting

Life is a canvas that accepts the brushstrokes of learning and adaptation. Every experience, every encounter is a chance to learn, to grow, and to adapt. Embracing new challenges, absorbing fresh knowledge, and adapting our views infuse vibrant hues into our canvas, creating a tapestry of resilience and understanding.

The Essence of Emotional Resilience

In the path of lifelong growth, we forge the shield of emotional resilience. We learn to weather life's storms without losing our roots. Like a tree that sways in the tempest but stands tall, we develop the resilience to bounce back from adversities, face relationship anxiety with courage, and fight overthinking with grace.

The Wisdom of Evolution

As we traverse the ever-changing landscapes of our lives, we grow, not just physically but emotionally and spiritually. Each phase and each experience adds to our evolution. We gather wisdom from our successes and tribulations, from the love we give and the love we receive. Through this evolution, we become seasoned navigators, skilled at steering the ship of our relationships through uncharted waters.

By committing to lifelong growth, we accept that the journey is the destination. It's a pledge to accept the twists and turns, the peaks and valleys, with an open heart and an open mind. It's a promise to cherish each step, each lesson, and each passing moment, for they are the building blocks of our unique, ever-evolving selves.

let us celebrate the eternal quest for personal improvement. Let us accept it as the heartbeat of our existence, for within this quest lies the promise of a life that is rich, meaningful, and abundantly fulfilling—a life that keeps flourishing, like the evergreen forest, for all eternity.

By accepting lifelong growth and self-improvement, we strengthen our emotional resilience and enrich our connections with others. As we continue our journey of growth and healing, let us remember that seeking support and investing in personal development are important steps toward cultivating healthier and more fulfilling relationships.

Chapter Eleven: Embracing a Life of Resilience and Love

In this Chapter, we reflect on the transformative journey we have undertaken to overcome relationship anxiety and overthinking. We explore the importance of cultivating resilience and self-love as we navigate the ups and downs of our relationships. By embracing a life of emotional strength and compassion, we create a foundation for lasting happiness and fulfillment in our connections with others.

The Art of Cultivating Emotional Resilience

In the vast landscape of life, emotional resilience is the sturdy vessel that helps us navigate through the storms and sail into calmer waters. It's the art of not merely enduring challenges but thriving in their midst, emerging stronger and wiser. In this section, we embark on a journey to understand the profound significance of cultivating emotional resilience—an art that fortifies not only ourselves but the very essence of our relationships.

Understanding Emotional Resilience

Emotional resilience is the fortress of the heart—the ability to weather the tempests of life while keeping our inner flame aglow. It's the capacity to bounce back from adversity, to transform pain into strength, and setbacks into stepping stones. With emotional resilience, we learn to surf the waves of change, maintaining a sense of balance and well-being.

Practicing Self-Care as a Foundation

Self-care is the cornerstone of emotional resilience. Just as a gardener nurtures the soil before planting seeds, we nurture ourselves to grow emotional strength. Regular exercise, sufficient sleep, a balanced diet, and moments of quiet reflection are the seeds of self-care. When we prioritize our well-being, we lay the foundation for emotional resilience to flourish.

Seeking Support and Connection

In the journey of building emotional resilience, we are not solitary travelers. We seek companionship and support along the way. Sharing our burdens, fears, and joys with loved ones creates a safety net of understanding and empathy. A listening ear, a comforting hug, or words of encouragement can bolster our emotional strength, reinforcing our resilience.

Engaging in Joyful Pursuits

Joy is the elixir that fuels emotional resilience. Engaging in activities that bring us genuine happiness and fulfillment—whether it's painting, hiking, cooking, or simply spending time with loved ones—recharges our emotional batteries. Joy acts as a catalyst, propelling us through challenges and aiding in quicker recoveries.

Positive Mindset and Healthy Responses

Emotional resilience is reflected in our mindset and responses to challenges. A positive outlook, an optimistic perspective, and healthy coping mechanisms are the building blocks. Instead of dwelling on the problem, we focus on solutions, cultivating resilience that allows us to approach challenges with grace and determination.

By cultivating emotional resilience, we carve a pathway to face relationship anxiety and overthinking with unwavering strength. It's the empowering force that turns adversity into an opportunity for growth. As we forge steel from the fires of life's challenges, we emerge with a heart that is more compassionate, a mind that is more open, and relationships that are more enduring.

let us celebrate the art of cultivating emotional resilience. Let us embrace the storms and the calm alike, for within this resilience lies the promise of a life that is deeply rooted, resilient, and flourishing—a life that stands tall, unshaken, and abundant in love.

Fostering Self-Love and Self-Compassion

In the grand tapestry of life, self-love and self-compassion are the warm, embracing arms that hold us close. They are the nurturing soil that allows love to blossom, not just for others but for ourselves. In this section, we embark on a heartfelt journey to understand the transformative power of self-love and self-compassion—a journey that unfurls not just within, but in the way we connect with the world and the people we cherish.

The Foundation of Self-Love

Self-love is the cornerstone of a fulfilling and authentic life. It's the acknowledgment of our worthiness, the gentle embrace of our strengths and weaknesses, and the unwavering belief in our inherent value as human beings. Just as we love our dear ones, we too deserve our love—a love that is unconditional, nurturing, and infinite.

Practicing Self-Compassion

Self-compassion is the gentle balm that soothes our souls. It's the art of treating ourselves with the same kindness and understanding we readily offer to our loved ones. When we stumble, when we falter, self-compassion whispers, "You are human, it's okay." It's a compassionate voice that silences the harsh criticism within and allows us to heal and grow.

Embracing Imperfections

In the dance of self-love, we embrace our imperfections as a cherished part of ourselves. Perfection is an illusion, and the pursuit of it is a futile endeavor. Instead, we celebrate our uniqueness, our quirks, and our flaws. Through self-love, we learn that imperfections are the brushstrokes that make our life's canvas truly beautiful and authentic.

Breaking Free from Self-Judgment

Self-judgment is the weight that shackles us to the ground, preventing us from soaring. Self-love is the liberating force that breaks those chains. As we cultivate self-love, the grip of self-judgment loosens. We learn to be kind to ourselves, to embrace our journey without harsh critique, allowing us to step forward with confidence and grace.

Authentic Connections through Self-Love

Self-love is the foundation upon which we build meaningful relationships with others. When we love and honor ourselves, we attract relationships that mirror this love and respect. We set healthy boundaries, we communicate our needs with assertiveness, and we engage in connections that nurture and enrich our lives.

By fostering self-love and self-compassion, we plant seeds of love that bloom into a garden of authenticity and fulfillment. It's a journey that begins within, radiating outward, touching the lives of those we hold dear. In the end, the love we have for ourselves is the blueprint for the love we share with the world.

Nurturing Lasting Love and Happiness

In the vast tapestry of relationships, love, and happiness are the vibrant threads that give it color and form. Yet, these threads require diligent care, nurturing, and weaving to create a masterpiece that withstands the test of time. In this section, we embark on a journey to understand the profound significance of nurturing lasting love and happiness—a journey that weaves together the threads of connection, shared experiences, and continuous communication.

Shared Experiences: The Glue of Connection
Shared experiences are the threads that weave the fabric of togetherness. They are the moments that resonate with laughter, tears, and growth. Whether it's a quiet evening by the fireplace or an adventure in a distant land, these experiences become the glue that binds hearts. Through shared experiences, we create a treasure trove of memories that light the path of our journey together.

Acts of Kindness: Love's Tender Gestures
Acts of kindness are the brushstrokes of love on the canvas of relationships. A kind word, a warm embrace, a thoughtful gesture—these simple acts carry immense weight. They are the language of love, a testament to our affection and care for our partners. Acts of kindness water the garden of love, allowing it to blossom and flourish.

Continuous Communication: The Lifeline of Love
Communication is the lifeline that keeps the heart of a relationship beating. It's not just about words, but the genuine desire to listen, understand, and connect. It's about expressing our feelings, sharing our dreams, and navigating challenges together. Through open and honest communication, we build bridges of trust, laying the foundation for a love that is enduring.

Investing in Emotional Fulfillment

Investing in the emotional well-being of our relationships is akin to nurturing a garden. We water it with love, patience, and understanding. Healthy relationships are wellsprings of emotional fulfillment. They provide us with a source of joy, support, and comfort, enriching our lives in immeasurable ways.

The Ripple Effect of Happiness

Happiness is a ripple that expands, touching not just us but all those around us. When we nurture lasting love and happiness within our relationships, we create a positive ripple effect. The joy and contentment we feel extend to our families, friends, and communities, contributing to a happier, harmonious world.

As we continue on our path of growth and healing, let us remember that our journey is not finite. Relationships require ongoing effort and self-awareness, and it is through this continuous dedication that we create the loving and supportive connections we desire.

Embrace the lessons learned in this book, and let us move forward with resilience and love, forging a path of fulfillment and happiness in our relationships. May our journey inspire others to overcome relationship anxiety and overthinking, fostering a world of healthier and more loving connections.

Conclusion

In this journey of overcoming relationship anxiety and overthinking, we have explored the depths of our emotions and thought patterns. We have gained valuable insights into the roots of our anxieties and insecurities, recognizing how past experiences and attachment styles shape our present relationships. Armed with this knowledge, we have embarked on a transformative process of healing and growth.

Throughout this book, we have delved into practical techniques and strategies to manage our emotions effectively. By cultivating self-awareness and mindfulness, we have learned to observe our thoughts and reactions with compassion and clarity. We have challenged negative thought patterns, reframing them with positive affirmations and realistic perspectives. Seeking professional support and engaging in personal growth have been essential in deepening our understanding of ourselves and our relationships.

We have also explored the importance of building trust and security in our connections. By embracing vulnerability, practicing open communication, and setting healthy boundaries, we have fostered emotional intimacy and a sense of safety in our relationships. We have learned the value of compromise, flexibility, and gratitude, reinforcing the bonds with our partners.

As we continue on our journey, we embrace a life of resilience and love. We understand that challenges and conflicts are inevitable, but we approach them with emotional strength and a willingness to grow together. By prioritizing self-love and self-compassion, we break free from the shackles of self-doubt and embrace our inherent worthiness.

Our journey does not end here. It is a continuous and transformative process of self-discovery and personal growth. As we move forward, we carry with us the wisdom and insights gained from this journey, building a foundation of healthier and more fulfilling relationships.

Let us face the future with confidence and optimism, embracing the joys and challenges that come our way. May we create a world of love, understanding, and compassion, nurturing connections that bring us closer to ourselves and others.

Remember, you have the power to overcome relationship anxiety and overthinking. Embrace the journey, and may it lead you to a life of love, fulfillment, and profound emotional connections.